published by

National Center for Youth Issues

ncyi.org

Practical Guidance Resources
Educators Can Trust

www.ncyi.org

W9-CNI-281

To Mali and A.J.
–Julia

Duplication and Copyright

No part of this publication may be reproduced, stored in a retrieval system
or transmitted in any form by any means, electronic, mechanical, photocopy,
recording or otherwise without prior written permission from the publisher
except for all worksheets and activities which may be reproduced for a specific
group or class. Reproduction for an entire school or school district is prohibited.

P.O. Box 22185
Chattanooga, TN 37422-2185
423.899.5714 • 800.477.8277
fax: 423.899.4547
www.ncyi.org

ISBN: 978-1-931636-49-0
© 2009 National Center for Youth Issues, Chattanooga, TN
All rights reserved.

Written by: Julia Cook
Illustrations by: Anita DuFalla
Published by National Center for Youth Issues
Softcover

Printed by RR Donnelley, Inc.
Reynosa, Mexico
July, 2011

Bobbette was a big, bad bully.

She made sure all the kids
at my school knew that

SHE was the boss.

She'd tell all of us what to do…

and we'd do it.

She'd tell all of us where to go…

and we'd go there.

She'd even tell all of us what to say…

and we'd say it.

If we didn't do what Bobbette told us to do, she'd look at us with her mean eyes. We all knew what that meant…

"If you don't do exactly what I say…

I'll twist you into a human pretzel!"

she'd tell us.

We all thought about what it would be like to be twisted into a human pretzel…and it scared us – a lot! So, we all ended up doing exactly what Bobbette told us to do, and we let her be the boss.

Bobbette liked to pick on kids, especially Winston.
Winston is the smartest kid in our whole school.

Bobbette made Winston do all of her homework.

Bobbette made Winston give her all of his lunch money.

Bobbette liked to make Winston cry…

and then she'd call him a crybaby.

Bobbette teased Winston every day. She said that
if he didn't do exactly what she told him to do…
she'd twist him into a human mini-pretzel!

Nobody liked the way Bobbette treated Winston,
but we were all too afraid to do anything about it.

Bobbette didn't have any real friends, but she didn't know that. Nobody liked Bobbette, but we pretended to like her so that she wouldn't show us her mean eyes.

Last week, Bobbette asked me to go over to her house after school. I didn't really want to go, but I went anyway. When we got to her house, her big brother Larry started bullying her!

HE told her what to do...
and she did it.

HE told her where to go...
and she went there.

HE even told her
what to say...
and she said it.

Larry made Bobbette cry...and then he called her a crybaby.
He told her that if she didn't do his homework for him, he'd twist her into

a human pretzel!!!!

"I don't ever have time to do my own homework," she whispered to me. "That's why I make Winston do it for me."

For the first time in my life, I started to feel sorry for Bobbette. I started to understand why she was so mean to everybody.

That night I went home and told my mom all about Bobbette.

I told her how mean she is to all of us and how mean her brother Larry is to her.

"Sounds like you have a true-blue bully on your hands," my mom said. "I'll get out the Bully Beans!"

"Bully Beans? What are you talking about?"

My mom reached into our kitchen cupboard and pulled out a bag of jelly beans. She grabbed a magic marker and wrote "Bully Beans" across the bag.

Bully Beans are magic jelly beans that when chewed up, remind kids that THEY have the power to stop bullies.

The "beans" in Bully Beans stands for

"**Bullies Everywhere Are Now Stopped!**"

"If you want to stop a bully, you have to take away their power. To do that you need to work together. Never hang out on the playground by yourself. Always stay with your friends in groups. Bobbette may be able to bully one of you, but I bet she won't try to bully all of you at once."

"When Bobbette picks on Winston, where do you and your friends stand?"

"Right next to Bobbette," I said.

"Why is that?" asked my mom.

"We don't want her to use her mean eyes on us," I said.

"Next time, tell everyone to stand right next to Winston. Tell them to look Bobbette right in the eyes."

**"That sounds scary!"
I said.**

"It won't be," said my mom, "as long as you eat a Bully Bean before you do it!"

"Another way to take away Bobbette's power is to stay away from her. Bobbette can't bully you if she can't communicate with you. If she tries to stare at you with her mean eyes, don't look at her. If she tries to come close to your group, ignore her and walk away."

"What if that doesn't work?" I asked.

"Tell everyone in your group to turn and face Bobbette. Have them stand up straight and tall and look her right in the eyes. Use your loud voice and tell Bobbette to

"BACK OFF!"

Say it so loud that
the entire school can
hear you!"

"That sounds scary!"
I said.

"It won't be," said my mom, "as
long as you eat a Bully Bean before
you do it.

"What if she tries to twist me into a
human pretzel?" I asked.

"Bobbette may think that she can twist one of you into a
pretzel, but she knows she can't twist all of you."

"Chances are if you are loud enough, one of the
teachers on the playground will hear you and come
to see if you need help."

"Why don't teachers stop kids who are bullying?" I asked.

"Teachers do stop them when they see it happen. The problem is that most bullies are very smart and they just don't get caught."

Mrs. Skundrich, Tony hits Josh at lunch.

"It's always a good idea to tell a teacher or a counselor when you see bullying. If you are too scared to tell them in person, write them a note and don't sign your name."

"Finally," she said, "it is very important for you to remember that Bobbette may be a bully on the outside, but on the inside, she's just a kid like you. If she ever decides to stop being a bully, give her a chance to become one of your real friends."

I couldn't believe the words I was hearing!

Me and Bobbette…real friends? NEVER!

The next day, I went to school and passed out the Bully Beans to all of my friends and talked to them about everything my mom had told me.

We all agreed to give the BULLY BEANS a try.

Just before the bell rang that morning,
Bobbette headed straight for Winston.

"Give me my homework, Squirt!" she demanded.

Everyone chewed up a Bully Bean and swallowed it. Then we all crowded around Winston.

Winston closed his eyes and swallowed his bean. "No," he squeaked back at her in a very high voice.

"What did you just say to me?" she asked him.

Winston looked up at Bobbette's mean eyes and said, "NO! Do your own homework!"

Bobbette couldn't believe her ears. Her mean eyes got bigger and meaner than I have ever seen them before.

She was just about to grab Winston by the collar, when our teacher came to the door and told us to come inside.

During class that morning, Bobbette tried glaring at Winston, but Winston wouldn't look at her. He just sat in his seat smiling and eating Bully Beans. I bet he ate about 20 of them!

When recess finally came, everyone ate another Bully Bean and headed for the door. Winston was the first one outside. Bobbette tried to run right after Winston, but we got to him first and stood right next to him.

"Hey squirt," she said.
"Get over here!!! NOW!"

Winston popped another Bully Bean into his mouth and chewed it up. We all walked away pretending not to hear Bobbette.

She chased him down,
mean eyes and all.

"If you don't stop right now, I'm going to twist you into a human mini-pretzel,"

she said.

We all stopped, turned around, stood up straight and tall, and stared right into Bobbette's mean eyes.

"Back off Bobbette!" I said with a very loud voice.

"We are sick and tired of you telling us all where to go!"

"We are sick and tired of you telling us all what to do!"

"We are sick and tired of you telling us all what to say!"

"We are sick and tired of your mean eyes, and your human pretzel threats, and most of all…we are sick and tired of you!!!!!"

I couldn't believe what I was saying!

The words just poured out of my mouth!

Bobbette took a step toward me.

"BACK OFF!"

I screamed.

"LEAVE US ALONE!"

Our recess teacher heard me scream and
came running over to us.

"Is everything OK?"
she asked.

I looked Bobbette right in the eyes, but this time
instead of having mean eyes, her eyes looked scared.
Her face turned white. She was in shock!

"Everything is fine,"
I said.

Bobbette looked up to our teacher and nodded in
agreement. Then she turned around slowly and
walked away.

When I got home, I told my mom what happened at school.

"Bully Beans really aren't magic, are they?" I asked.

"Not exactly," said my mom. "They're just regular old jelly beans that taste good. Their only magic is that they helped you find the courage inside yourself to stand up to Bobbette."

After that day, Bobbette stopped telling all of us what to do.

She stopped **telling all of us where to go.**

She stopped **telling all of us what to say.**

She stopped **looking at us with her mean eyes.**

And she hasn't said another word since
about twisting us into human pretzels.

Yesterday, Bobbette hung around our group for the very first time.

She was nice to everyone, even Winston.

I don't think she will ever become one of my friends, but at least things are better than they used to be.

Winston told Bobbette all about the Bully Beans.

He even gave her a few of them so she could try them out on her big brother Larry.

She told him she'd need more...

probably about 20!